Loan Mods Made Easy

BRIAN J. MILLER

Disclaimer & Legal Notice

All requests should be sent to:
Brian J. Miller
385 Court St. Suite 202
Plymouth, MA 02360

The subject matter of this book was written by me using the knowledge that I have acquired over the years by actually doing loan modifications. Although I have done my best to insure the accuracy and completeness of this book I make no warranties or guarantees with respect to the accuracy or completeness of the contents of this book. I make no warranties or guarantees either written, stated, or implied for the contents of this book or the intended results. The advice, examples, templates, and strategies given in this book may not be suitable for your situation and I encourage you to consult an attorney when appropriate. I am not an attorney and I am not attempting to give legal advice in this book. I shall not be held liable for any real or consequential damages or losses that may occur to the user of this book. Results are not guaranteed. Please check with your state for applicable laws, as they do vary by state.

This book is available in print form or as an e-book at Amazon.com or LoanModsMadeEasy.net

ISBN-13: 978-0615619484

TABLE OF CONTENTS

DO IT YOURSELF

LOAN MODIFICATION

Loan Mods Made Easy

Brian Miller is an investor, realtor, and lender mediator based in America's Hometown of Plymouth, Massachusetts. Experienced in real estate marketing, property management, short sales, and loan modifications, Brian has the background and expertise to make a significant difference in the lives of many homeowners. Since 2006, Brian has helped many clients solve their real estate problems through short sales and loan modifications. Additionally, Brian also offers help with credit restoration in the aftermath of financial difficulties.

This DIY manual shares proven techniques that will enable you to complete your own loan modification with ease and confidence.

INTRODUCTION

My Burning Desire

Because you're interested in this book, I'm sure that you've personally been affected by this current economic crisis. I know how personal it is for you, as it is also personal for me. The only thing stopping you now is your fear. When you finish reading this booklet, it is my burning desire that this fear is gone and that you immediately take action.

This doesn't have to be you!
A successful loan modification can help you save your home from foreclosure.

In our economic history, we've never seen so much wealth evaporate so quickly. Of the approximate 16 million Americans who bought homes between 2004 and 2006, most find themselves upside down with little or no equity, as do those who have recently refinanced. The experts say that 8 to 10 million homes will go into foreclosure by 2012, and that the second wave of foreclosures has yet to come. This will be driven by the "not quite prime" adjustable rate mortgages that banks loaned to borrowers during the housing boom.

Many loan modifications are not being approved today. However, this booklet will arm you with the right information and tools to ensure that you can successfully structure and submit a loan modification package. Always remember - it's all about knowledge and taking action.

Never in history have the banks and government implemented programs for distressed homeowners to keep their homes. This is a once in a lifetime opportunity. Seize the moment and ensure your own success!

Brian J. Miller

CHAPTER ONE

"Whenever one door closes, a new one always opens."

- Helen Keller

Loan Modification 101

If you are really upside down (more than 50%), you may want to do a short sale and walk away; it just may not make financial sense for you to keep your home. This is a personal decision, but some homes that were purchased or refinanced recently may never come back to their original purchase values in our lifetime!

As we go along through this manual, you will see that the most common type of loan modification HAMP (Home Affordable Modification Program – see Chapter 5 for more information), which has strict and steadfast rules for qualification. However, we deal with lots of lenders on a daily basis and have found that their criteria for non-HAMP modifications seem to vary. Thankfully, this means if you cannot qualify for a HAMP loan, you still have options out there – and the terms of these alternative programs are often easier to negotiate because the lenders have more flexibility than they do with HAMP.

The Top Ten Guidelines for Loan Modification

1: Being Late is Okay

Yes, it is possible to get a modification without being late on your payments, but it's not easy. Do the math. If you were the lender, which applications would you put on the top of the file - the ones who would probably go to foreclosure and cost them thousands, or the ones who are paying every month? If you're hung up on your FICO score you're probably going to have to decide which is more important. Enough said.

2: The HAMP Guidelines

In order to qualify for a HAMP modification, your PITI (Principal, Interest, Taxes, Insurance) must be more than you 31% of your gross monthly income. Your total debt DTI (Debt to Income) ratio seems to work best if it falls between 90-110% of your gross monthly income. We'll talk more about this later. If you do not fit HAMP guidelines, your lender may have other plans available.

3: Type of Loan

An adjustable rate mortgage (ARM) or a negative amortization rate loan has the best success in being converted to fixed rate loans. All others are fair game and will be considered for a loan modification.

4: Hardship

What has changed since you took your loan?

- Divorce or separation from spouse or partner
- Loss of income
- Reduction of income
- Illness (you, spouse, or family member)
- Military service
- Death of spouse/partner, co-borrower, family member
- Disability

If you or a loved one experienced a lengthy or severe illness that contributed to your financial hardships, most lenders will take this into consideration when reviewing your application.

Ideally, you are now in a position to pay for a modified loan even if you previously were unable to make payments.

Let's face it, in this economy there's no shortage of hardship out there. Your lender needs to know specifically what your hardship is. If you don't have a hardship your lender will be reluctant to modify your loan. Their guidelines state that if you default on your payments without a hardship simply to qualify for a modification, you are ineligible. This is called a "strategic default" and will get you nowhere. On the other hand, if you are current in your payments, you can and should still apply, but don't expect a great modification. The best scenario is that you had a hardship but now have the ability to repay a modified loan. See Chapter 3 for more information.

5: Occupant

HAMP is for owner-occupied properties only. These are the easiest modifications. Rental properties – even those with HELOC (Home Equity Line of Credit) loans – can be modified using the lender's own plans.

6: Age of Loan

HAMP guidelines state that your loan must have been taken out before 2009.

7: P&L (Profit and Loss) Statement

If you have other assets beyond the property, this could become an issue. It may have to be discussed with your lender, so be prepared for that.

8: Ability to Pay

You will have to demonstrate to the lender that you have the ability to repay a modified loan. Please refer back to the above ratios in Guideline #2 for more information.

9: Status

FDIC guidelines state that the borrowers must have not filed for bankruptcy during the life of the loan and a foreclosure sale must not be imminent. However, borrowers have indeed obtained modifications after bankruptcy or in the face of foreclosure. The guide also encourages borrowers to apply even if they are not late on payments, but do not be discouraged if you are behind – people in your position have received modifications even when applicants who are current are not getting good offers themselves.

10: The top 3 Qualifiers

- **A.** Ability to repay
- **B.** Hardship
- **C.** Your loan is an ARM or negative amortization product

A and **B** = Likely to get a loan modification

A, **B**, and **C** = Very likely to get a loan modification

Chapter One Recap

If you decide that you want to apply for a loan modification, remember that applicants who are now in a position to repay their loan but who have struggled in the past due to hardship and/or the type of loan they had are the most likely candidates. Lenders want to see that you had legitimate reasons for not being able to manage your original loan *and* that you will not be a risk to them should they approve your loan modification.

CHAPTER TWO

"There's a difference between interest and commitment. When you are interested in doing something, you do it only when circumstances permit. When you're committed to something, you accept no excuses, only results."

– *Art Turock*

Why Do Your Own Loan Modification?

1. You have help.

Federal and state agencies have been staffed and contracted to help you with the loan modification process. Hundreds of millions of dollars of tax money has been allocated to these agencies to provide counseling. If needed, you may find these resources truly helpful.

2. Who cares more than you?

Anybody you contact for assistance should be strictly in *your* corner and look out for your best interest, which is often not the case. Read on...

a. Government Modification Programs

While all these government agencies provide a wealth of information, they do very little as far as helping you take action; they were also established to help represent lenders and homeowners, and therefore are not looking out for you alone.

b. Lenders

The lenders also are not on your side, and will most likely try to get you to accept a deal that clearly benefits them.

c. Loan Modification Companies

Lastly, be careful of any for-profit loan modification companies; they are in it for the money. Many of these companies are out-of-work sub-prime loan brokers. However, if you decide to go that route, you will at least now have the knowledge to assist you in picking the right company.

If you do decide to hire someone, I would suggest a local attorney with loan modification experience. They are governed by their local BAR association, and also are most likely concerned about their reputation in the community.

Forensic Loan Audits

You've probably heard about these audits to identify RESPA and TILA violations (Real Estate Settlement Procedures Act and Truth in Lending Act) in your loan. Just about all loans have violations of some kind or another. Do you think that your lender cares if you threaten to sue? They are obviously a better-funded and better-prepared opponent; as such, I do not recommend taking this route – it is an unfair match and you most likely will not get the outcome you want even if you are in the right!

2. Human Touch

Although the customer reps, negotiators, and underwriters are on the other team, you also have to remember that they are people just like you. They are working hard just like the rest of us; they also have bills and mortgage payments. Always try to establish a connection with everyone with whom you speak. Not only is this good karma, it may help you down the line to have a well-established rapport with those assisting you!

3. Don't Over Think It!

Your loan modification may take a while and you may have to keep sending in updated paperwork, but it's not difficult. Keep it simple and keep it stupid. You will succeed!

Chapter Two Recap

Sometimes, *you* are the only person whom you can rely on and trust. With a polite, professional attitude and the guidance from the many resources available – including this book! – you *can* get through the process of applying for your loan modification.

CHAPTER THREE

"A pessimist is one who makes difficulties of his opportunities and an optimist is one who makes opportunities of his difficulties."

– Harry S. Truman

Qualifying for a Loan Mod

HAMP - Home Affordable Modification Program

This program is the "holy grail" of modifications, and the one for which you should apply. Please go to www.loanmodsmadeeasy.net to use our free qualification calculator.

HAMP was started by the Obama administration in 2009, and is slated to end December 31, 2013. HAMP is the most beneficial to homeowners as well as servicers, as they are paid $1000 on inception of the modification and $1000 per year for up to 3 years, as long as the payments are being made.

A few of the guidelines are:

- Owner occupied properties only
- Loan had to be made before January, 2009
- Loan must be less than $729,750
- Current payment (PITI) must be over 31% of gross wages
- Borrower must have suffered a hardship
- The new payment (PITI) must be no more than 31% of gross income
- New payment must include PITI – principal, interest, taxes, and insurance

To assist the borrower in qualification, the program features these remedies:

1. Interest rate to be lowered to 2% for the first 5 years
Interest rate will be approx. 3-4% for years 5-8 *
Interest rate for years 8-end of term to be at current rates

2. The term can be extended for up to 40 years

3. A portion of the principal balance is to be stripped out via a principal reduction or balloon payment. The balloon payment is to be paid at the end of the loan. This balloon note doesn't accrue interest and must be paid in one payment at the end of the note.

The qualifying criteria work in the order above. In other words, if they can't get you to 31% of gross income using the rate, they should then use the 2% rate along with a longer term. If the combination of these two doesn't work then they should then use these two along with a principal reduction or balloon note.

If you qualify for HAMP your lender may offer you a 3-month "trial modification." This is a precursor for a permanent modification but not a guarantee of approval. It may also go longer than the standard 3 months.

- Remember, if you don't qualify for HAMP most lenders do have in-house programs. The qualifications and terms will vary, but they all seem to be using the 31% rule.
- Please see denials in Chapter 7

* After 5 years HAMP rules say that you must be adjusted from 31% to 38% of your gross income when you were first approved. This adjustment is done through an interest rate increase.

Chapter Three Recap

Created as a safety line for those about to lose their homes, HAMP has helped many families avoid foreclosure. The qualification guidelines for this program are very rigid, but don't be discouraged if you are ineligible – lenders offer other types of non-HAMP loan modifications for which you may qualify.

CHAPTER FOUR

"There is one quality which one must possess to win, and that is definiteness of purpose, the knowledge of what one wants, and a burning desire to possess it."

\- *Napoleon Hill*

The Application

1. Pull your credit reports from the three major bureaus (TransUnion, Equifax, and Experian) from www.annualcreditreport.com for free once per year. You should address information for current bills only on your financial statement - credit cards and loans that you are not currently paying do not need to be put on your financial statement. Be ready to explain anything that is on your report.

2. Before you apply, make sure that you don't have a checking or savings with your lender. If you do, think about changing it to a different bank – generally, it's not a good idea for your lender to have your emergency money. Be aware of mergers such as Country Wide to Bank of America, Wachovia to Wells Fargo, WAMU to Chase, and so on. As an example, let's say you took your mortgage with Country Wide but you have a savings account with Bank of America.

You should think about moving your savings account to another bank before you apply.

3. Gather these documents for each borrower:

- Last two paystubs
- Last two months' checking (all pages) and savings account statements
- Latest utility bill (gas or electric only)
- Copy of homeowners insurance coverage
- Copy of property tax bill
- Completed RMA form (Request for Modification and Affidavit) and hardship letter
- Completed Dodd-Frank certificate
- Completed 4506-T EZ Form
- Last two years' tax returns (all pages). If you didn't file, include a letter explaining why and preferably a copy of your application for extension form
- YTD P&L (Profit and Loss) statement for self employed
- Hardship letter (See samples in Appendix)

Hardship Letter Tips

This letter should be handwritten. Try to keep your hardship letter to 250 words or less. If you write illegibly, write it anyway for effect but also submit a typed version. Don't be long-winded here. Describe your hardship, when it happened, and how you now have the ability to make a lower payment. Even if your spouse/partner is not a co-borrower on the loan, a reduction in his or her income is considered a hardship.

4. Make sure that all of your documents have a page number and your loan number on each page, and include table of contents with your application. The table of contents should follow your cover letter, which should state your name, property address, mailing address (if different), email address, loan number, and your best phone contact number. You should briefly state what you're applying for – preferably the HAMP and a principal balance reduction.

5. It's time to call your lender now (I know it may seem scary, but not to worry - you now have the knowledge!) Simply say that you are having difficulty making monthly payments due to a hardship that you have experienced. Say, "I/We really want to keep my/our home and am/are wondering if you have any programs that may help me/us?" They will probably ask you about your

hardship and your financial sheet, which you should have in front of you. It's okay to answer these questions, but do not say more than you have to. Keep your answers short and to the point. When finished, get the fax number for sending in your application.

Don't EVER call your lender without your financial sheet in front of you, as you do not want to seem ill prepared.

Chapter Four Recap

The application process itself may seem complicated, but as long as you are prepared with knowledge of your credit report and history, have ensured that your bank accounts are not affiliated with your lender, and have all necessary documents on hand, you are ready to call. Remember to be polite and professional – treat person on the other end of the line the way that you want to be treated in turn!

CHAPTER FIVE

"Go for it now. The future is promised to no one."

– Wayne Dyer

Follow Up

Follow up is HUGE! When you read the newspapers about all the rejected applications, keep in mind that lack of follow up is a major reason that so many applicants are turned away.

Initial Call

Your first follow up should be in 4-5 business days. Call the lender and ask:

- Did you receive my package?
- Do you need any other documents?
- Is my file in the system?
- Is my package complete?
- Has it been assigned?
- Your name?
- Your ID number?

After this first call, follow up should be done at least once per week. You must always ask:

- Is there a sale date scheduled? (only if you are behind)
- Has my package been assigned to a negotiator?
- When do you expect it to be assigned?
- Do you need any other documents?

When you follow up ALWAYS note the date, the contact person's name, and what you spoke about. When you do get assigned to a negotiator, be certain to get his or her name and direct contact info.

Chapter Five Recap

Weekly follow up is the key. Be sure to ask pertinent questions and write down date, name of person with whom you spoke, and answers to your questions. Remember - the squeaky wheel gets the grease!

CHAPTER SIX

"Our thinking and our behavior are always in anticipation of a response. It is therefore fear-based."

- Deepak Chopra

Negotiations

When calling make sure that you have a great attitude! If you get a bad agent, politely end the call, and call back later. Always have your loan number and social security number on hand, as you will be asked for it.

HAMP's terms are pretty much set in stone and are therefore non-negotiable but you should always:

- Be a good listener. Listen more and talk less.
- Have empathy. Most of these lender employees work in a high pressure, low pay situation for long hours. They are working folks just like you with bills and mortgages to pay.
- Understand the negotiator's needs, and not just yours. They want to complete and close your file in as little time as necessary so they can get paid and move on.

- Be prepared. Know your strengths and weaknesses on your application. This will help you with your decision on whether to accept their first offer.
- Ask for more than you want, whether it is a better rate, term, principal reduction, or balloon payment. Make your request realistic so as to not damage your credibility.
- If you have to give in on something, ALWAYS get something in return.
- ALWAYS rehearse what you're going to say and understand what your goal is before you call.

You don't need to be a magician to get a fair loan modification – you just need to be knowledgeable, prepared...**and have strong negotiating skills!**

Ask for concessions! These are examples of requests for concessions that we've seen others use:

1. "The low interest rate that you are offering for the initial 5 years is very helpful but the payment is still higher than I'm comfortable with. Is there any way that we can extend the term or look at a principal reduction?"

2. "Can we extend the initial 5 year term to 10 years? This would help me to get to the point where the property may be appreciating again, and I can finally afford to sell."

3. "The offer doesn't get me to where I hoped to be. Is there any way we can get it to X per month?"

4. "After the initial period, is there any way that the investor will give me a fixed rate for the duration?"

5. "Instead of stepping my rate up at once after the initial period, could we step it up gradually each year over time?"

6. "My property value continues to slide. Is there any way that the investor could approve a lower rate? I've heard of rates as low as 2%."

7. "The economy and housing market seems to be getting worse. I want to keep this property and ride it out but I'm so under water sometimes I wonder if it's worth it. Is there any way that the investor would consider a principal reduction?"

8. "The way the rental market is in my area, I need a little more cushion for vacancy. Is there any way the investor could help me there?"

Chapter Six Recap

Remember that if you are applying for a HAMP loan, there isn't much room for negotiating the terms of your modification. However, lenders have more flexibility with other types of loan modifications, so don't be afraid to negotiate!

CHAPTER SEVEN

"We are continually faced by great opportunities brilliantly disguised as insoluble problems."

– Lee Iacocca

Approvals and Denials

Approved

Congratulations, your application has been approved!

Carefully read the approval terms and if acceptable sign, date, notarize (sometimes), make copies for yourself, and send back via overnight mail with certified funds (if needed). Make sure that you do this within the allotted time, because one day late will have you starting all over again. Please make sure to call to verify receipt of your overnight package.

Second Mortgages

Once you've mailed back your approval package, it's time to deal with that pesky second mortgage. Phone them and ask them what they need for the application packet. Follow the procedures in this book – you're an expert by now –

and send the package to them. Bear in mind that most second lien holders are in a very risky position, especially if your first mortgage is for more than your house is worth. This means that they may be willing to settle with you for less than what is owed. If you've defaulted on your second mortgage for at least 5 months, this is the time to negotiate; around the 6th month mark most lenders charge off the note and pass it along to a collection agency. This time, then, is when they are the most motivated. It is not uncommon for second mortgages to be settled for 10-30% of what's owed and sometimes with favorable payment terms.

Once you've started negotiations don't be in a hurry. Time is on your side if you don't have lots of equity in your home.

If talks stall, one statement that we like to make is "My attorney and I are weighing out my/our options. We are discussing bankruptcy* or a short sale. Is there anything that you can do to help me/us avoid this?"

*Second mortgages are usually wiped out in a bankruptcy and very little is paid to the lender in a short sale. They want to avoid this!

Denied

Relax, up to 90% of all modification packages and 50% of all trial modifications are denied. Most of them are denied due to poor applications. If you invested in this book and followed its instructions, that's probably not the reason.

1. You may need to ask up to 5 different times for a reinstatement review. Hopefully you get a different agent every time, until one of them says yes. If you can't get an agent to reinstate, use finesse and politely ask to speak to a manager. Ask why it was rejected, and apply for a reinstatement review. Remember to be humble. You are asking for help.

> **Script Examples**
>
> "I/We believe that we meet the guidelines for HAMP. Why haven't I/We been offered a trial modification program?"
>
> "I/We have run into a road block with our application. Would you please ask your loss mitigation department to review my/our file again?"

2. Send a Qualified Written Request (see glossary and example), to the CEO, legal department, and loss mitigation department.

3. You may also send an additional Qualified Written Request to the loss mitigation and the legal department asking:

- Is the note backed by either Fannie Mae or Freddie Mac?
- Can I have a copy of the note?
- Can I have a list of transactions pertaining to the note?
- What is the name of the investor?
- Has the investor received TARP (Trouble Asset Relief Program) funds?

4. Call your local congressman/congresswoman and ask them to send you his or her letter of request form. Fill it out and send it back and he or she will write a letter on your behalf.

These are guidelines for action you should take if you are denied. Use your discretion and take it one step at a time.

Chapter Seven Recap

Hopefully, if you reasonably fit the lender's qualifying guidelines and have followed the steps in this book, you have been approved for your loan mod and are ready to tackle your second mortgage. If, however, you've been denied for any reason, continue speak with the lender and politely but firmly request a review of your application.

APPENDIX

I. Explanation of Application Documents

Remember to include your loan number on ALL documents!

1. Paystubs

- Include if you're a W-2 employee
- If you're a 1099 or Self-Employed, you will need copies of cancelled checks

2. Checking and Savings Account Statements

- Checking and Savings account deposits must always be consistent with your state of gross income on your financial form. If you qualified at $4000 per month on the application, your deposits must be that monthly.
- Deposits averaged over a 3-6 month period are fine.
- The income amount stated on your application must remain consistent with your monthly bank deposits for the duration of the process. This is key!

3. Last Utility Bill

Gas or electric only!

4. Homeowners' Insurance

Include declaration page only.

5. Property Tax Bill

Include even if your lender is paying taxes.

6. RMA (Request for Modification and Affidavit) Form*

A. For Pension/401K, put N/A. It's none of their business unless you're using it for income.

B. Don't leave blank spaces. If it's N/A, put N/A.

C. For alimony or child support, you need to include any court documents.

D. If paid bi-weekly, multiply by 26 and divide by 12 to determine your monthly income.

E. List only minimum credit card payments due and only on cards that you are currently paying.

F. If you're not paying on your second mortgage, put N/A.

G. Your debt-to-income ratio is calculated by dividing your total monthly household gross income into your total monthly expenditures.

7. Dodd-Frank Certificate

Answer questions, sign, and date.

8. 4506-T EZ

Fill in 12/31/10, 12/31/09, 12/31/08, sign, and date.

9. Last 2 Years' Tax Returns

- Include for all borrowers.
- If you didn't file, include a letter explaining why, and preferably a copy of your IRS request for extension form.

10. YTD Profit and Loss for Self-Employed

- Always put the name of your company at the top of the page.
- Include at the end of the P&L "I attest that the information given above is true and correct." "Signed under the pains and penalties of perjury."
- Sign and date.

*If you have rooms or apartments that you rent in your home, 75% of your gross rental income can be used as your personal income. You will need leases and cancelled checks to prove this.

You can add income for someone who is not on the loan such as significant other or someone who is willing to help you financially. They may write a contribution letter stating how much and how long they are willing to help. You should have this letter notarized and submit your contributor's recent paystubs or savings account statements along with it.

II. Application Cover Sheet Sample

ATTENTION: LOAN MODIFICATION DEPARTMENT

To: Bank of America

Fax: 800-520-5019

Re: Loan Number xxxxxxx

Borrower's Name: xxxxxxxx

Subject Property: xxxxxxx

Dear Sir or Madam:

I/we am/are applying for a HAMP loan modification. I/we are seeking payment relief through a reduced interest rate, longer term, principal reduction, and/or any combination of these remedies.

Included, please find:

(1)	Cover	1 Page	Pages 1
(2)	RMA	2	2-3
(3)	Acknowledgement and Agreement	1	4
(4)	Hardship Letter	1	5
(5)	Dodd-Frank Certificate	1	6
(6)	4056-T EZ	1	7
(7)	Cur Haz Ins Dec Page	1	8
(8)	Cur Prop Tax Bill	1	9
(9)	Utility Electric Bill	1	10

(10)	Pay Stubs	2	11-12
(11)	W2 2010	1	13
(12)	2009 Tax Returns	3	14-16
(13)	2010 Tax Returns	3	17-19
(14)	2011 YTD P&L	1	20
(15)	2 Months' Bank Statements Mar/Apr	18	21-38

TOTAL PAGES **38**

If you have any questions, please contact me by phone at xxx-xxx-xxxx or email at xxxxx@xxxxxx.com.

Sincerely,

xxxxxxxxxxx

III. Hardship Letter Samples

The following hardship letters have slightly different headings and closings. As long as your information is clearly displayed on the letter, you can vary the format of your letter.

Sample 1 – Reduced Income and Family Illness

Bank of America
Loan # xxxxxxxxxxxx
Mr. and Mrs. xxxxxxx
xxxxxxxxxxxxxxxxxx

December 10, 2010

To Whom It May Concern:

I am writing to explain the unfortunate circumstances that have made it extremely difficult for my wife and I to stay current on our adjustable rate mortgage. It is our hope that, considering our recent struggles, you will work with us to help us keep our home.

Last year, my mother fell ill and moved in with us so that we could care for her. Not only has this situation taken an emotional toll, it has required me to cut back significantly on my hours at work and switch into a part-time position. While my wife still works fulltime as a manager, the reduction in my income, coupled with the added costs of caring for my mother, has made it nearly impossible to come up with our recently adjusted higher mortgage payment.

My wife and I still have secure jobs, so I can assure you that we can make a monthly payment. However, because we will not be able to continue to pay our current amount, we are asking that Bank of America consider switching us to a low fixed rate mortgage so that we can keep our home and remain current in our payments.

We very much appreciate your time and understanding. Please contact me with any questions or to discuss our application further.

Sincerely,
xxxxxxxx

Sample 2 – Loss of Income

To: Wells Fargo Mortgage
Re: Mortgage Modification for Ms. xxxxxx, Account # xxxxxxxxx

October 1, 2010

Dear Sir or Madam:

I am writing to ask for your understanding and assistance in helping me keep my home.

Seven months ago, I lost my job as an administrative assistant because my employer had to downsize significantly. Thankfully, I had enough savings that I was able to continue making my mortgage payment for three months. For the past four months, however, I have not been able to pay in full, and I am aware that I am at risk of losing my home to foreclosure.

Thankfully, I was recently able to find a new job with comparable pay. However, getting four months behind in my mortgage and other bills has created an insurmountable obstacle, and I cannot get back on track. I have been consistent in my payments for the, so it is my hope that this recent setback will not cause me to lose my home.

Because of my improved financial situation and ability to pay my mortgage again, it is my hope that we can work together to reduce the delinquent amount and lower my payment so that I can get back on track. My savings is depleted and I have no other options at this point. With so many homeowners experiencing similar hardships, Wells Fargo hopefully can understand my struggles and help me keep my home.

Thank you, and I hope to hear from you soon to discuss my application for a loan modification.

Sincerely,

xxxxxxxxxx

Sample 3 – Divorce, Loss of Spousal Income

Account no. xxxxxxxx
Mr. xxxx xxxxxx

July 3, 2011

To: CitiFinancial Mortgage

I am applying for a loan modification so that my children and I can remain in our home. With my recently increased interest rate and my current personal and financial struggles, I have fallen behind and am afraid that I will lose my home to foreclosure.

This past year has been extremely difficult, as my wife and I separated and recently made the decision to move forward with our divorce. Because I have retained custody of our children, we agreed that I would continue to live in our home so as not to disrupt their lives any further.

My wife's income was necessary to make ends meet between our mortgage, car payments, student loans, and more. On top of this reduction in household income, I also am paying spousal support as part of our divorce agreement, which makes it even more difficult to stay current. On the positive side, I still have secure employment, and I am confident that I can make a lowered monthly payment.

The financial security of my family has always been important to me, and falling behind on my payments for the past two months was stressful and embarrassing. I hope that CitiFinancial Mortgage will take into account my previously strong credit and track record when reviewing this application for a loan modification. My family has been through enough this year, and it would be devastating to lose our home on top of everything else.

I look forward to working with you, and hope to hear from you soon.

Yours Truly,

xxxxxxxxxxx

Sample 4 - Illness, Disability

May 27, 2009

To Whom It May Concern:

Please consider my application for a HAMP loan modification.

Last year, I had heart surgery that forced me to retire from my teaching position before I was eligible for my full retirement benefits. While I am receiving disability payments and a portion of my pension, my income is still lower and I cannot continue to pay my mortgage. HAMP guidelines state that an applicant's payment must be greater than 31% of his or her gross income – mine is currently 43%. Between my mortgage and my health care costs, I will not be able to keep my home for much longer without a modification.

I thought about selling when I realized that I would not be able to continue to make payments, but because my home's value has lowered since I bought it six years ago, I would walk away with nothing, and I cannot afford to do that right now.

If we could rework the terms of my loan and potentially reduce my principal balance so that my monthly payment is lower, I would be able to stay in my home despite my financial setbacks. Additionally, I would not be in as deep underwater as I am now that my home has devalued.

I appreciate any assistance you can provide, and look forward to speaking with you regarding my application. Please let me know if you need any further information.

Sincerely,
xxxxxxxx
Account number xxxxxxx

IV. Profit and Loss (P&L) Statement Sample

Year to Date Profit and Loss Statement

XYZ Company

1/1/10-9/30/10

INCOME	
Commissions:	22,100
Rental Income:	20,040
TOTAL INCOME:	42,140
EXPENSES	
Motor Vehicle:	2,315
Gasoline:	1,520
Tolls:	41
Insurance:	722
Repairs:	302
Meals:	520
Phone:	603
TOTAL EXPENSES:	6023

NET PROFIT: $36,117

I/We attest that the information given above is true and correct under the pains and penalty of perjury.

________________________ ________________________

Borrower Co-Borrower

V. Sample Letter Explaining Failure to File Taxes

October 17, 2010

Chase Fulfillment Center

4500 Cherry Creek Dr South, Suite 960

Glendale, CO 80246

Re: Loan Number xxxxxxxxxxxx

Dear Sir or Madam:

I have not yet filed federal or state tax returns for the years 2007, 2008, and 2009. I expect to do so as soon as my funding for tax preparation allows.

As always, I appreciate your consideration and understanding in this matter.

Sincerely,

xxxxxxxxxxxx

VI. Forms

You can easily find the RMA, Dodd-Frank, and 4506-T EZ forms by searching online or by clicking the links listed on http://www.makinghomeaffordable.gov/get-assistance/request-modification.

VII. Glossary

4506-T/4506-T EZ: This is titled Request for Transcript of Tax Return and is typically used to determine an applicant's creditworthiness, particularly when applying for a mortgage

Adjustable Rate Mortgage (ARM): A mortgage in which the interest rate on the note is periodically adjusted based on a specific index

Amortization: The process by which the borrower's principal decreases over the life of a loan

Annual Percentage Rate: The annual interest rate charged by a lender for borrowing money

Applicant: The person applying for a loan

Application Package: All relevant documents required for a particular type of application; see Chapter Three for more information on what is required for a loan mod application package

APR: (See "Annual Percentage Rate")

Balloon Payment: A large lump sum paid at the end of a loan that has not amortized fully during its life

Bankruptcy: The legal status of an individual or organization unable to pay its debts

Certified Funds: Payment that is guaranteed to clear by the company issuing the funds; examples include Cashier's Check or Money Order

Collection: The actions of a creditor attempting to reclaim debts owed

Collection Agency: An agency hired by a creditor to settle debt with individuals or businesses

Credit Bureau: A company that collects and reports information on consumers; the three major credit bureaus are Experian, Equifax, and TransUnion

Credit Report: A report on a consumer's credit history used to determine creditworthiness

Credit Score: A numerical expression based on an analysis of a person's credit history used to determine creditworthiness

Debt-to-Income (DTI) Ratio: The ratio of one's monthly debt to his or her monthly income – the higher the ratio, the riskier the consumer is generally considered

Default: Occurs when a debtor has not met the agreements stated in the terms of a loan such as not making payments on time

Disability: A physical, mental, emotional, or personal hindrance to one's ability to work, make payments, or meet other obligations

Dodd-Frank Certification: A legal document required by mortgage assistance programs certifying that the applicant has not been convicted of (a) felony larceny, theft, fraud, or forgery, (b) money laundering or (c) tax evasion.

DTI: (See "Debt-to-Income Ratio")

Equifax: One of three major credit bureaus; see "Credit Bureau" for more information

Equity: The difference between the value of a home and what is owed on the mortgage

Experian One of three major credit bureaus; see "Credit Bureau" for more information

Fair Isaac and Company: (see "FICO")

Federal Deposit Insurance Corporation: (See "FDIC")

FDIC: An independent government agency that insures and guarantees the safety of deposits in member banks

FICO: A major credit scoring company that calculates creditworthiness based on payment history, use of credit, length of credit, and more

FICO Score: The score generated by FICO based on the above information; scores range from 300-850

Financial Statement: The formal record of the financial activities and history of an individual or business

First Mortgage: A first mortgage has priority over any other liens on a property and therefore is considered lower risk; if the borrower defaults, the first mortgage lender has first rights to the property

Fixed Rate Mortgage: A mortgage in which the interest rate on the note remains fixed over the period of the loan

Foreclosure: The process by which a bank or lender repossesses property due to the borrower's failure to make mortgage payments

Forensic Loan Audit: An analysis of original loan documents, usually by a lawyer or lawyer software, to catch any predatory lending violations

HAMP: A government loan modification program introduced in 2009 designed to help homeowners avoid foreclosure

Hardship: A personal hindrance to one's ability to remain current on mortgage or other payments

Hardship Letter: A letter to the lender explaining the circumstances of the applicant's hardship; see examples in Appendix

HELOC: (See "Home Equity Line of Credit")

Home Affordable Modification Program: (See "HAMP")

Home Equity Line of Credit: Loan in which the lender agrees upon a maximum amount in a specified term and where the collateral is the borrower's equity in his or her home

Homeowners Insurance: Property insurance protecting an individual's home against damages to the house or possessions within the home

Income Reduction: Loss of income; can be considered a hardship even if it is the spouse's income that has been reduced

Interest: The fee charged by a lender for the use of borrowed money, usually expressed as an APR or annual percentage rate

Interest Rate: The particular rate charged by a lender for the use of borrowed money, usually expressed as an APR or annual percentage rate

Investor: The lender's source of money

Late Payment: A payment submitted by the borrower after the due date agreed upon with the lender

Lendee: The person or business borrowing and receiving loan funds; the borrower

Lender: The person or company loaning funds to a borrower

Lien: A legal claim over property intended to secure payment of debt

Loan: Funds issued to and borrowed by a person or business, creating a debt that must be repaid according to established agreements

Loan Modification: A process by which the original terms of a mortgage are renegotiated and modified, generally because the borrower is experiencing difficulty making payments

Loss Mitigation Department: A third party or division within a bank that handles the negotiations between a homeowner and the lender

Loan Modification Company: A for-profit company that assists borrowers in the process of applying for and acquiring a loan modification

Loan Negotiator: Handles negotiations between the borrower and the lender to determine the terms of a loan

Loan Repayment: The repayment terms agreed upon by the borrower and the lender

Loan Originator: Assists consumers in preparing the application and beginning the loan process

Loan Underwriter: Evaluates and approves or denies a loan request submitted by applicant

Market Value: Amount for which property can be sold in a given market

Negative Equity: Occurs when the value of property is less than the amount owed

Negotiator: (See "Loan Negotiator")

Notarize: To have a document certified and legalized by a notary public

Notary/Notary Public: Person authorized to certify legal documents

Note: A written promise or agreement to repay a loan

Originator: (See "Loan Originator")

Owner-Occupied Property: Lived in by the owner (as opposed to a rental property)

PITI: Mortgage payment that is the sum of the principal, interest, taxes, and insurance

P&L Statement: (See "Profit and Loss Statement")

Positive Equity: Occurs when the value of property is more than the amount owed

Predatory Lending: Describes deceptive or fraudulent practices of lenders during the loan origination process

Prime Mortgage: A classification of mortgages carrying a low risk because they are issued to very creditworthy borrowers

Principal: Sum of a debt not including interest; the original amount borrowed

Principal Balance Reduction: An agreement between the lender and borrower to reduce the amount of the principal owed; see "Principal"

Principal, Interest, Taxes, Insurance: (See "PITI")

Profit and Loss Statement: Summary of profits and losses for a self-employed individual or business over a specified period of time

Property Value: Appraised value of property, usually the market value

Qualified Written Request: An account inquiry by the borrower protected by RESPA (See "RESPA") addressing a specific issue or concern and using the following recommended format:

I am writing because:

- *Describe the issue or the question you have and/or what action you believe the lender should take.*
- *Attach copies of any related written materials.*
- *Describe any conversations with customer service regarding the issue and to whom you spoke.*
- *Describe any previous steps you have taken or attempts to resolve the issue.*
- *List a daytime telephone number in case a customer service representative wishes to contact you.*
- *They have 20 days to acknowledge receipt of your request and 60 days to take action.*

Real Estate Settlement Procedures Act: (See "RESPA")

Rental Property: Rented out by the owner to a tenant (as opposed to owner-occupied property)

Repayment Plan: The repayment terms agreed upon by the lender and borrower to ensure that a loan amortizes within its term

Request for Modification and Affidavit: (See "RMA Form")

RESPA: An Act prohibiting undisclosed kickbacks between lenders, real estate agents, settlement service agents and other companies associated with the buying and selling of property; protects the consumer from "bait and switch" tactics

RMA Form: Provides information to the lender about the borrower's financial situation and any hardships

Second Mortgage: A mortgage taken out on a property that is already mortgaged; considered higher-risk because the first mortgage has primary rights over the property

Short Sale: A sale in which the proceeds will be less than any liens against the property and the owner cannot afford to repay the full amount of the liens; the lien holders agree to accept less than the amount owed

Strategic Default: A decision by a borrower to stop making payments despite being able to do so in order to default on the loan

Subprime Mortgage: A classification of mortgages carrying a higher risk because they are issued to less creditworthy borrowers

TARP: A program authorizing government purchase of assets and equity from financial institutions

Term: The period of time in which a loan agreement is in force and during which the loan must be repaid or renegotiated

TILA: A 1968 act requiring lenders to fully disclose terms and costs, thereby protecting borrowers and promoting informed consumer credit decisions

TransUnion: One of three major credit bureaus; see "Credit Bureau" for more information

Trouble Asset Relief Program: (See "TARP")

Truth in Lending Act: (See "TILA")

Underwriter: (See "Loan Underwriter")

Upside Down: Refers to a loan situation in which the borrower has negative equity and owes more than the property is worth

Year-to-Date (YTD): The period beginning January 1st of the current year and ending today

Made in United States
Orlando, FL
07 November 2026

90339164R00043